My United States

Ohio

MARTIN GITLIN

Children's Press®
An Imprint of Scholastic Inc.

Content Consultant

James Wolfinger, PhD, Associate Dean and Professor
College of Education, DePaul University, Chicago, Illinois

Library of Congress Cataloging-in-Publication Data
Names: Gitlin, Marty, author.
Title: Ohio / by Martin Gitlin.
Description: New York, NY : Children's Press, an imprint of Scholastic Inc., 2018. | Series: A true book | Includes
   bibliographical references and index.
Identifiers: LCCN 2017048737 | ISBN 9780531235683 (library binding) | ISBN 9780531250877 (pbk.)
Subjects: LCSH: Ohio—Juvenile literature.
Classification: LCC F491.3 .G55 2018 | DDC 977.1—dc23
LC record available at https://lccn.loc.gov/2017048737

Photographs ©: cover: Cindy Hopkins/Alamy Images; back cover bottom: Clarence Holmes/age fotostock; back cover ribbon: AliceLiddelle/
Getty Images; 3 bottom: Americanspirit/Dreamstime; 3 top: Jim McMahon/Mapman ®; 4 top: chas53/iStockphoto; 4 bottom: Madlen/
Shutterstock; 5 top: Diamond Images/Getty Images; 5 bottom: vikif/iStockphoto; 7 center top: Maria Feklistova/Dreamstime; 7 center
bottom: csfotoimages/iStockphoto; 7 top: Grigor Atanasov/Dreamstime; 7 bottom: Richard Cummins/robertharding/Superstock, Inc.; 8-9:
Ron Sanford/Science Source; 11 background: Tom Till/Superstock, Inc.; 11 inset: James Adkins/EyeEm/Getty Images; 12: Douglas Sacha/
Getty Images; 13 main: Shiell Richard/Animals Animals; 13 inset: Madlen/Shutterstock; 14: KeithBinns/iStockphoto; 15: Waynebridge/
Dreamstime; 16-17: traveler1116/iStockphoto; 19: U.S. Bureau of Engraving and Printing; 20: Tigatelu/Dreamstime; 22 left: cbies/
Shutterstock; 22 right: Nicku/Shutterstock; 23 center right: chas53/iStockphoto; 23 top left: imagenavi/Getty Images; 23 top right:
Natikka/iStockphoto; 23 bottom left: Courtesy of the Ohio History Connection; 23 center left: Shackleford-Photography/iStockphoto; 23
bottom right: ShoreTie/iStockphoto; 24-25: Andy Marlin/AM Photography/Getty Images; 27: NativeStock/North Wind Picture Archives;
29: MPI/Getty Images; 30 right: Mary Evans Picture Library/age fotostock; 30 left: Andy Marlin/AM Photography/Getty Images; 31 top:
NBC NewsWire/Getty Images; 31 bottom right: Everett Collection/age fotostock; 31 bottom left: Nicku/Shutterstock; 32: Bettmann/Getty
Images; 33: Hagen Hopkins/Getty Images; 34-35: Holly Hildreth/Getty Images; 36: Diamond Images/Getty Images; 37: AFP Contributor/
Getty Images; 38: Karen Schiely/MCT/Newscom; 39: Andre Jenny/Alamy Images; 40 inset: Chicago Tribune/Getty Images; 40 background:
PepitoPhotos/Getty Images; 41: WENN Ltd/Alamy Images; 42 top left: The Granger Collection; 42 top right: Bettmann/Getty Images; 42
bottom left: Library of Congress/Getty Images; 42 center right: TopFoto/The Image Works; 42 bottom right: Album/Superstock, Inc.; 43
top left: Ian T. Horrocks/Getty Images; 43 top right: Dick Loek/Getty Images; 43 bottom left: Rue des Archives/The Granger Collection; 43
bottom right: Alison Buck/Getty Images; 43 center right: Patrick McMullan/Getty Images; 43 bottom right: Jason Miller/Getty Images;
44 right: Lambert Carol Jean Something New Under the Sun Merrimack Media Cambridge MA. 2014/Scott.bigham/Wikimedia; 44 bottom
left: Drozhzhina Elena/Shutterstock; 44 top left: vikif/iStockphoto; 45 top left: National Baseball Hall of Fame Library/Getty Images; 45 top
right: Ingram Publishing/Newscom; 45 center: Cannon Films/Album/Superstock, Inc.; 45 bottom: Hagen Hopkins/Getty Images.

Maps by Map Hero Inc.

All rights reserved. Published in 2019 by Children's Press, an imprint of Scholastic Inc.
Printed in North Mankato, MN, USA 113

SCHOLASTIC, CHILDREN'S PRESS, A TRUE BOOK™, and associated logos are trademarks and/or registered trademarks of
Scholastic Inc.

Scholastic Inc., 557 Broadway, New York, NY 10012

1 2 3 4 5 6 7 8 9 10 R 28 27 26 25 24 23 22 21 20 19

Front: Rock & Roll Hall of Fame

Back: Ohio State Fair

Welcome to Ohio

UNITED STATES

Ohio

Find the Truth!

Everything you are about to read is true *except* for one of the sentences on this page.

Which one is **TRUE**?

T or F Famous astronauts Neil Armstrong and John Glenn were both from Ohio.

T or F The state bird of Ohio is the robin.

OHIO
BIRTHPLACE OF AVIATION
XTREEMS

Find the answers in this book.

3

Contents

THE **BIG** TRUTH!

Cardinal

What Represents Ohio?

Buckeye nuts

Cleveland Indians

Lemonade Lucy

This Is Ohio!

MICHIGAN

LAKE ERIE

PENNSYLVANIA

Marblehead
Lighthouse

TOLEDO

Maumee

American Civil War
Museum of Ohio

African Safari
Wildlife Park

SANDUSKY

Sandusky

Edison Birthplace
Museum

Cedar Point
Amusement Park

CLEVELAND

Cuyahoga

Rock and Roll
Hall of Fame

YOUNGSTOWN

AKRON

Neil Armstrong
Air & Space Museum

Scioto

Wyandot Popcorn
Museum

OHIO

CANTON

Pro Football
Hall of Fame

Schoenbrunn Village
State Memorial

INDIANA

SunWatch Indian Village/
Archaeological Park

Ohio Statehouse

Muskingum

Appalachian Plateau

DAYTON

The Horseshoe,
Ohio State University

COLUMBUS

Dayton Aviation
Heritage National
Historical Park

Great Miami

Cincinnati Zoo &
Botanical Garden

Scioto

Hocking Hills
State Park

Ohio

WEST VIRGINIA

CINCINNATI

Cincinnati
Museum Center

Ohio

KENTUCKY

N
W   E
S

0   30
Miles

6

1 Cedar Point

Every summer, millions of people flock to this amusement park in Sandusky to ride some of the tallest and fastest roller coasters in the world.

2 Rock and Roll Hall of Fame

This Cleveland landmark is home to exhibits about the history of popular music. Visitors can check out musical instruments and other artifacts that belonged to legendary artists such as the Beatles, Stevie Wonder, and Nirvana.

3 Dayton Aviation Heritage National Historical Park

This attraction is dedicated to Orville and Wilbur Wright, the brothers who built the first airplane. These pioneers of flight were originally from Ohio.

4 Cincinnati Museum Center

Several museums are all located in a single building near downtown Cincinnati. Here, visitors can check out hands-on science activities, exhibits about local history, and more.

There are more than 74,000 farms in Ohio.

Ohio is home to several Amish communities, which follow a strict Christian religion. Among them is this farm in Doughty Valley.

CHAPTER 1

Land and Wildlife

Ohio is at its most beautiful each year when summer gives way to fall. In stunning shades of red, yellow, and green, the changing colors of the leaves provide some of the prettiest **foliage** in the United States. However, Ohio is more than just trees. It also has everything from **bogs** to waterfalls. In the state's major cities, skyscrapers tower high above the ground. All across the state, there are incredible sights to behold.

The Great Outdoors

Ohio features a wide variety of landscapes. The northern Great Lakes Plains region features fertile **lowland**. Sandy beaches run along the shores of Lake Erie. Central and western Ohio feature large plains that are ideal for farming. The Bluegrass Region of south-central Ohio is notable for its deep valleys and small caves. On the Appalachian Plateau in eastern Ohio, hills rise more than 1,000 feet (305 meters) into the air.

This map shows where the higher (orange) and lower (green) areas are in Ohio.

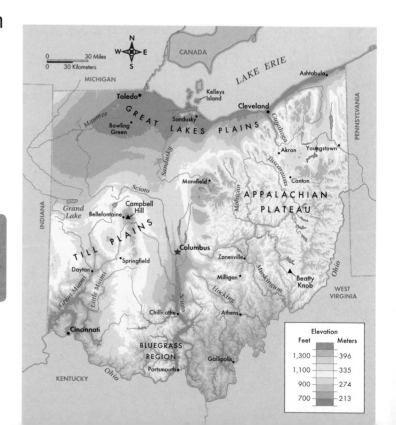

A Serpent and a Crystal

Among Ohio's most notable landmarks is the Serpent Mound Impact Crater. Some scientists believe it was formed by a meteor crash millions of years ago. The crater is named for Serpent Mound, a snake-like earthen mound built inside of it by Native Americans centuries ago.

Another amazing natural attraction can be found in the Ohio Caverns. Inside the caverns is Crystal King, a mineral deposit that hangs like a huge icicle. Crystal King is nearly 5 feet (1.5 m) long and weighs about 400 pounds (181 kilograms).

Rock formations in the Ohio Caverns

What's the Temperature?

Ohio is warm in the summer and cold in the winter. In general, the southern region is just a bit warmer than the north. The average temperature is about 52 degrees Fahrenheit (11 degrees Celsius) in northern Ohio and 55°F (13°C) in the south. This slight temperature difference helps lead to more snowfall in the north. More than twice as much snow falls in the Cleveland area as in Columbus or Cincinnati.

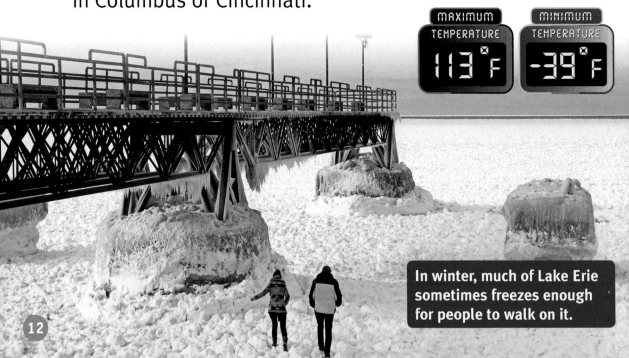

MAXIMUM TEMPERATURE
113°F

MINIMUM TEMPERATURE
-39°F

In winter, much of Lake Erie sometimes freezes enough for people to walk on it.

Growing Wild

It makes sense that the state tree of the "Buckeye State" is the buckeye. This tree produces buckeye nuts, which are similar to chestnuts. They can be eaten only if shelled and roasted. They are poisonous when raw! Other common trees include beech, aspen, and American elm. Another is the pawpaw, which produces a unique edible fruit. Ohio is filled with other plants, too. Wildflowers such as trillium, aster, and wild lilies are among them.

Buckeye nuts grow inside spiny golden fruits.

Cool and Creepy Creatures

Spiders and bats are among the creatures that live in Ohio's many caves. Larger wildlife roam through the state's forests and hills. Animals that can be seen foraging for food throughout the state include black bears, coyotes, bobcats, and beavers. Also prominent is the white-tailed deer, which is the official state **mammal**.

Black bears disappeared from Ohio in the 1800s. Today, the bears are back, and their population is growing.

Ring-necked pheasants were originally brought from Asia to the United States in the late 1800s.

About 350 species of birds have been spotted throughout Ohio. Among the most interesting are ring-necked pheasants, wild turkeys, great horned owls, and red-headed woodpeckers. Blue jays and robins are very common in backyards and wild areas alike. Water snakes slither off the shores of Lake Erie near Cleveland. Frogs, newts, and toads hop across the state, while box turtles wander slowly through woodland areas.

Ohio's capitol was built mainly of Columbus's local limestone.

Government

Ohio's state capital, Columbus, is located almost right in the middle of the state. The cities of Zanesville and Chillicothe each served as Ohio's capital for short periods in the early 1800s. However, because of its central location, Columbus was chosen as the permanent capital in 1816. Today's Columbus is not only the center of government in Ohio, but also the state's largest city.

Three Branches

Ohio's government is made up of executive, legislative, and judicial branches. The governor heads the executive branch and appoints leaders of various state **agencies**. The legislative branch creates new laws that can be approved or **vetoed** by the governor. The judicial branch includes Ohio's courts.

OHIO'S STATE GOVERNMENT

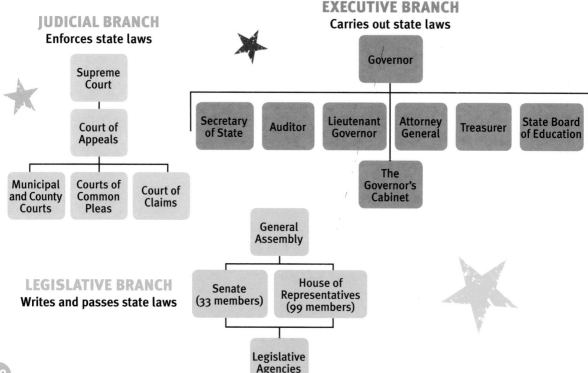

JUDICIAL BRANCH
Enforces state laws

- Supreme Court
- Court of Appeals
- Municipal and County Courts
- Courts of Common Pleas
- Court of Claims

EXECUTIVE BRANCH
Carries out state laws

- Governor
- Secretary of State
- Auditor
- Lieutenant Governor
- Attorney General
- Treasurer
- State Board of Education
- The Governor's Cabinet

LEGISLATIVE BRANCH
Writes and passes state laws

- General Assembly
- Senate (33 members)
- House of Representatives (99 members)
- Legislative Agencies

William Henry Harrison

Ulysses S. Grant

Rutherford B. Hayes

James Garfield

Benjamin Harrison

William McKinley

William Howard Taft

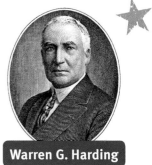
Warren G. Harding

Home of Presidents

Ohio is tied with Virginia for producing the most U.S. presidents of any state. Among them was William Henry Harrison, who spent less time in office than any other president. Harrison died after just 32 days as president. Many blame his passing on his inauguration speech in 1841. Harrison spoke for nearly two hours on a freezing March morning. He developed pneumonia and died a month later.

Ohio in the National Government

Each state elects officials to represent it in the U.S. Congress. Like every state, Ohio has two senators. The U.S. House of Representatives relies on a state's population to determine its numbers. Ohio has 16 representatives in the House.

Every four years, states vote on the next U.S. president. Each state is granted a number of electoral votes based on its number of members of Congress. With two senators and 16 representatives, Ohio has 18 electoral votes.

2 senators and 16 representatives

18 electoral votes

With eighteen electoral votes, Ohio's voice in presidential elections is above average.

The People of Ohio

Elected officials in Ohio represent a population with a range of interests, lifestyles, and backgrounds.

Ethnicity (2016 estimates)

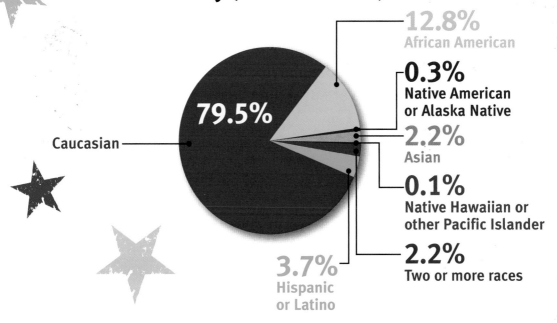

79.5% Caucasian

12.8% African American

0.3% Native American or Alaska Native

2.2% Asian

0.1% Native Hawaiian or other Pacific Islander

2.2% Two or more races

3.7% Hispanic or Latino

66% own their own homes.

78% live in cities.

26% of the population have a college degree.

89% of the population graduated from high school.

7% speak a language other than English at home.

THE **BIG** TRUTH!

What Represents Ohio?

States choose specific animals, plants, and objects to represent the values and characteristics of the land and its people. Find out why these symbols were chosen to represent Ohio or discover surprising curiosities about them.

Flag

Ohio's state flag is unlike any other in the country. It is a burgee. This means it has slanting sides with a triangular shape cut out at the end. All other state flags are rectangles. Like the U.S. flag, Ohio's flag features a red, white, and blue design of stars and stripes. The 17 stars on the flag represent Ohio's place as the 17th state.

Seal

Ohio's state seal shows a rising sun with 13 rays that symbolize the original 13 colonies. A sheaf of wheat in the foreground is a symbol of Ohio's bountiful farmland.

Red Carnation
STATE FLOWER
Ohio-born president William McKinley often wore a red carnation on his jacket for good luck.

Tomato Juice
STATE BEVERAGE
Tomato juice was adopted as Ohio's state beverage in 1965 to coincide with the Tomato Festival held in Reynoldsburg.

Black Racer
STATE REPTILE
This snake assists Ohio's farmers by killing rodents that damage crops.

Cardinal
STATE BIRD
This beautiful bird brightens all 88 of Ohio's counties, both in rural and urban areas.

Ohio Flint
STATE GEMSTONE
Large amounts of this gem can be found in eastern and central Ohio.

Bullfrog
STATE FROG
This frog's loud croaks can be heard coming from ponds, marshes, and slow-moving streams throughout Ohio.

The first humans in present-day Ohio hunted giant Ice Age animals such as the woolly mammoth.

CHAPTER 3

History

Ohio has been a state for more than 200 years. But that is only a small fraction of the time that people have made the area their home. Experts believe that people first came to what is now Ohio about 13,000 years ago. These early settlers probably came from Asia into what is now Alaska across a land bridge. As these hunters pursued large prehistoric animals, they made their way south across North America. Some of them ended up in present-day Ohio.

The First Ohioans

Archaeologists call the earliest people of Ohio Paleo-Indians. They were **nomads** who traveled frequently and hunted using handmade spears. Eventually, they started settling down and learning to farm. By about 800 BCE, the Adena culture had formed. Another culture, the Hopewell, developed around 100 BCE. The Hopewell were descendants of the Adena. They built huge earthen mounds and raised crops such as sunflowers, squash, and pumpkins.

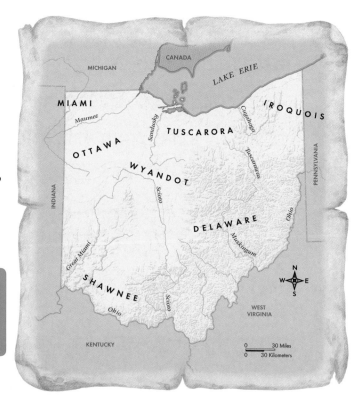

This map shows some of the major tribes that lived in what is now Ohio before Europeans came.

The Shawnee traditionally lived in villages of bark-covered houses.

The Next Generations

The Hopewell people disappeared from Ohio by around 400 CE. Disease, food shortages, or other threats may have killed them or forced them out of the area. Other cultures eventually moved into the area to take their place. Among them were the Delaware from the east, Iroquois from the north, and Shawnee from the south. As they settled in Ohio, other new people started to arrive from even farther away.

Trading and Fighting

In 1670, French explorers likely became the first Europeans to arrive in modern-day Ohio. France claimed the area, and its settlers established a fur trade with Native Americans. They were soon joined by the British. A fur trade rivalry soon began between the French and British settlers. As the Europeans moved in, many Native Americans were forced out of their homes.

This map shows routes European explorers took as they visited and settled what is now Ohio.

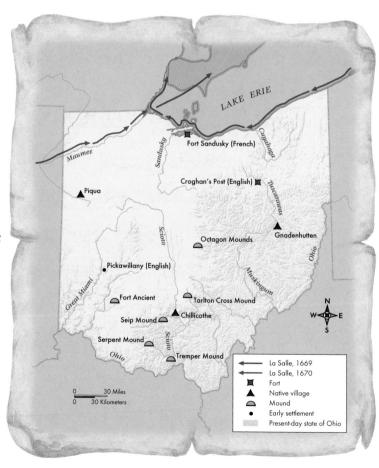

LAKE ERIE

Maumee

Sandusky

Fort Sandusky (French)

Cuyahoga

Croghan's Post (English)

Tuscarawas

Piqua

Scioto

Octagon Mounds

Gnadenhutten

Ohio

Pickawillany (English)

Muskingum

Great Miami

Fort Ancient

Tarlton Cross Mound

N

Seip Mound

Chillicothe

W E

Serpent Mound

Scioto

S

Ohio

Tremper Mound

0   30 Miles
0   30 Kilometers

⟵ La Salle, 1669
⟵ La Salle, 1670
▨ Fort
▲ Native village
⌒ Mound
• Early settlement
Present-day state of Ohio

Some Native Americans worked to stay out of the conflict during the Revolutionary War, but others fought alongside British or colonial forces.

The rivalry eventually led to the French and Indian War (1754–1763). Even with the area's Native Americans on their side, the French lost the war. They were forced to hand Ohio over to the British in 1763. Not long afterward, the Revolutionary War (1775–1783) began. America's colonists eventually defeated the British military and, newly independent, formed the United States of America.

Statehood and Beyond

In 1787, the U.S. Congress enacted the Northwest **Ordinance**. This law called for the creation of new states within what was known then as the Northwest Territory. As a result, Ohio was granted statehood in 1803. Roads, canals, and railroads lured settlers to Ohio as it grew to become the third most populous state in the country by 1840. Ohio soon became one of the top crop-producing states.

Timeline of Ohio Events

11,000 BCE
Ohio's first inhabitants have arrived.

1670
French explorers become the first Europeans to reach Ohio.

11,000 BCE > **400 CE** > **1670** > **1763**

400 CE
The Hopewell culture disappears from Ohio and several other Native American groups begin moving into the area.

1763
Great Britain takes control of Ohio after the French and Indian War.

Moving Forward

Ohio manufacturers played a leading role in the North's victory in the Civil War (1861–1865). European immigrants who moved to cities along Lake Erie helped Ohio become an industrial leader in the late 1800s and early 1900s. The result was a huge rise in the populations of cities such as Cleveland and Toledo. Ohio was becoming an increasingly urban state.

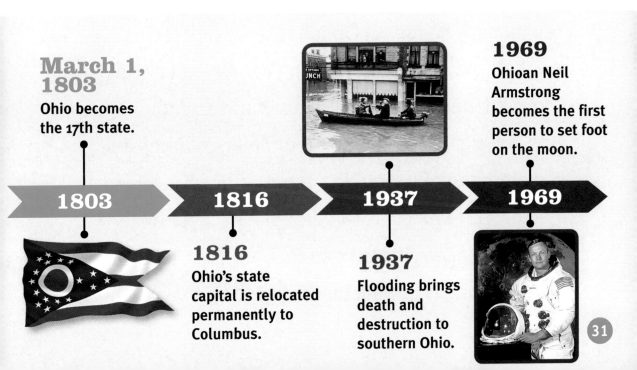

March 1, 1803
Ohio becomes the 17th state.

1803

1816
Ohio's state capital is relocated permanently to Columbus.

1816

1937

1937
Flooding brings death and destruction to southern Ohio.

1969
Ohioan Neil Armstrong becomes the first person to set foot on the moon.

1969

Carl Stokes was elected mayor in Cleveland twice before retiring from politics in 1971.

Modern Ohio

The modern history of Ohio has been marked by great accomplishments. Among the Ohioans who achieved greatness were Dayton natives Wilbur and Orville Wright. They completed the first successful powered airplane flight in 1903. In 1967, Cleveland elected Carl Stokes as the first black mayor of a major American city. Ohioan Neil Armstrong became the first person to walk on the moon two years later.

John Glenn

Neil Armstrong might not have traveled to the moon if another Ohio astronaut named John Glenn hadn't made history first. Glenn was born in the southeastern Ohio town of Cambridge and attended nearby Muskingum College. He joined the American space program in 1959 and was a member of the very first group of astronauts, called the Mercury Seven. He became the first American to orbit Earth in 1962. His next major mission was in politics. Glenn served in the U.S. Senate from 1974 to 1999. He died in December 2016.

The first Ohio State Fair was held in 1850. Today, the event draws more than 800,000 people each year.

Culture

Arts and culture abound in Ohio. Museums of art and natural history can be found in many of the state's cities. Writers, artists, and performers from Ohio have entertained people around the world. Plays, concerts, and other performances are held every day at venues across the state. Ohioans never have to worry about running out of things to do and see!

The Cleveland Indians played against the Chicago Cubs in the 2016 World Series.

Cheering for the Home Team

Cleveland and Cincinnati are the centers of professional sports in Ohio. The Cleveland Indians and Cincinnati Reds play Major League Baseball. The Cleveland Browns and Cincinnati Bengals compete in the National Football League. Basketball superstar LeBron James has spent most of his career leading the Cleveland Cavaliers. Hockey fans in Columbus root for the Blue Jackets. The capital city also hosts Ohio State University sports. Fans throughout the state embrace the dominant Buckeyes football team.

Fun Festivals

Every August, people with twin siblings head to the Twins Day Festival in Twinsburg. The event is a celebration of twins everywhere. It is just one of many annual fun festivals in Ohio. These often celebrate local edible treats, such as the Maple Syrup Festival in Oxford and the Country Applefest in Lebanon. The Ohio State Fair is held every year in Columbus, drawing massive crowds with live entertainment, rides, and more.

The Twins Day Festival has been held each year since 1976.

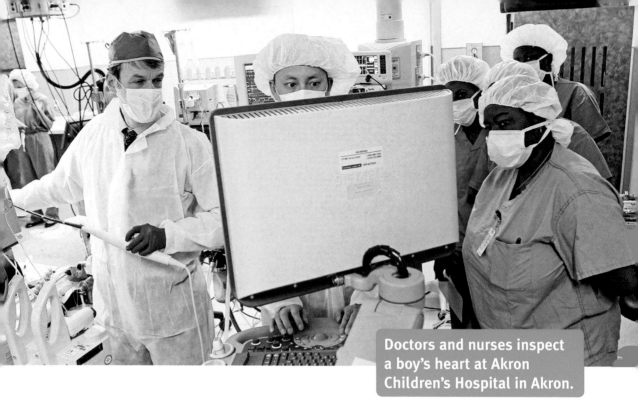

Doctors and nurses inspect a boy's heart at Akron Children's Hospital in Akron.

Jobs, Jobs, Jobs

More than five million Ohioans are employed. Many work in service professions. These jobs include nurses, teachers, waiters, and store employees. Transportation occupations such as truck and bus drivers are also popular in the state. A large number of Ohioans have jobs in factories, where they help make everything from car parts to house paint.

Shrinking Industries

The number of farms in Ohio has decreased over the years. As a result, fewer young people are entering this once-prominent profession. Only 7 percent of all Ohio farmers are 35 or younger. About three in 10 are at least 65 years old.

Farming is not the only industry that has taken a hit in Ohio. Many factories have shut down in recent decades, causing people to move away from industrial cities such as Cleveland and Toledo.

Even as farming technology rapidly improves, Ohio's Amish farmers still use traditional farming tools, such as horse-drawn carts.

Fabulous Food

Many regions of Ohio are famous for cooking up local specialties. Potato dumplings called pierogi are popular in Cleveland. In Cincinnati, people love to eat chili-topped spaghetti. The town of Barberton is known for its delicious fried chicken. Great food can be found wherever one travels in Ohio.

Cincinnati Chili

Ask an adult to help you!

This dish was made famous by the Skyline Chili restaurant chain in Cincinnati. Be sure to use the official Skyline brand chili, which contains chocolate and cinnamon!

Ingredients
1 can Skyline brand chili
Cooked spaghetti
Shredded cheddar cheese

Directions
Heat the chili in a small saucepan over medium heat. Serve over the spaghetti. Pile the cheese on top of the entire dish until you almost can't see the chili or pasta anymore. Enjoy!

Fiona the hippo, a young calf, is a favorite of visitors to the Cincinnati Zoo and Botanical Garden.

A State with a Lot of Heart

Ohio's slogan used to be "The Heart of It All." That's because the state is shaped like a heart. It is also because Ohio offers residents and visitors so much to do. The new slogan takes that spirit even further: "Ohio, So Much to Discover." The diversity of events, activities, and nature make the state a place for residents and visitors alike to enjoy, marvel at, and remember. ★

Famous People

Tecumseh

(1768–1813) was a Shawnee chief and political leader. He fought against U.S. attempts to force Native Americans out of Ohio.

Ulysses S. Grant

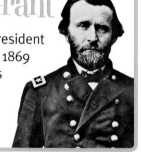

(1822–1885) served as president of the United States from 1869 to 1877. His leadership as general helped the North win the Civil War. He was born in Point Pleasant.

Thomas Edison

(1847–1931) is considered the greatest inventor in American history. This creator of the phonograph, motion picture camera, and long-lasting lightbulb was born in Milan.

Jesse Owens

(1913–1980) won four gold medals at the 1936 Summer Olympics in Germany, making him a hero around the world. He grew up in Cleveland and attended Ohio State University.

Doris Day

(1922–) is a singer and actress born in Cincinnati. She was among the top film stars of her generation and is also an animal rights activist.

Paul Newman

(1925–2008) was born and raised in a Cleveland suburb before emerging as a movie star and director. He won an Academy Award in 1987 for his performance in *The Color of Money*.

Erma Bombeck

(1927–1996) was an author and humorist. The Bellbrook native wrote about daily life in American suburbs for three decades.

Maya Lin

(1959–) is an artist and designer specializing in sculptures. Among the designs created by the Athens native is the Vietnam Veterans Memorial.

Steven Spielberg

(1946–) has directed and produced some of the most successful films of all time, including *Jaws*, *E.T. the Extra-Terrestrial*, and *Saving Private Ryan*. He was born in Cincinnati.

Nancy Cartwright

(1957–) is best known as the voice of Bart Simpson, the animated star of *The Simpsons*. Born in Dayton, she is also a television producer and author.

LeBron James

(1984–) is among the greatest basketball players ever. He led the Cleveland Cavaliers to their only NBA championship in 2016. He was born in Akron.

Did You Know That . . .

Ohio native Rutherford B. Hayes, who was the 19th president of the United States, refused to allow alcohol to be served in the White House. As a result, his wife, Lucy Hayes, became known as "Lemonade Lucy" for the nonalcoholic beverages served to visitors.

Americans can thank Niles resident Harry M. Stevens for putting the first hot dog on a bun. As a concession stand worker at New York Giants baseball games, Stevens created the popular cookout and ballpark food for fans in the early 1900s.

John Lambert of Ohio City built the first gas-powered automobile in the United States in 1891. The car could travel only 5 miles (8 kilometers) per hour. Lambert was born in Champaign County in 1860.

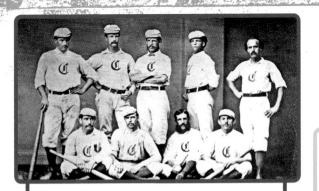

The Cincinnati Red Stockings became the country's first professional baseball team in 1869. They challenged anyone that would dare play them that year and won all 57 games they played.

The cash register was invented by James J. Ritty of Dayton in 1879. He came up with the idea to prevent employees from stealing money from his business.

Comic book hero Superman was a Cleveland creation. Writer Jerry Siegel and artist Joe Shuster came up with the legendary character.

Did you find the truth?

 T Famous astronauts Neil Armstrong and John Glenn were both from Ohio.

 F The state bird of Ohio is the robin.

Resources

Books

Bailer, Darice. *What's Great About Ohio?* Minneapolis: Lerner Publications, 2016.

Kavanagh, James. *Ohio Nature Set: Field Guides to Wildlife, Birds, Trees & Wildflowers.* Dunedin, FL: Waterford Press, 2017.

Rozett, Louise (ed.). *Fast Facts About the 50 States: Plus Puerto Rico and Washington, D.C.* New York: Children's Press, 2010.

Santella, Andrew. *The French and Indian War.* New York: Children's Press, 2012.

Stille, Darlene R. *Ohio.* New York: Children's Press, 2015.

Visit this Scholastic website for more information on Ohio:
★ www.factsfornow.scholastic.com
Enter the keyword **Ohio**

Important Words

agencies (AY-juhn-seez) government departments that provide services to the public

archaeologists (ahr-kee-AH-luh-jists) people who study the distant past, often by digging up old buildings, objects, and bones and examining them carefully

bogs (BAHGZ) areas of soft, wet land

foliage (FOH-lee-ij) the leaves of a tree or other plant

lowland (LOH-land) an area of low elevation

mammal (MAM-uhl) a warm-blooded animal that has hair or fur and usually gives birth to live babies

nomads (NOH-madz) members of a community that travels from place to place instead of living in the same place all the time

ordinance (OR-duh-nuhns) a law or regulation, especially one for a town or city

vetoed (VEE-tohd) stopped a bill from becoming a law

Index

Page numbers in **bold** indicate illustrations.

About the Author

Martin Gitlin is an educational book author based in Cleveland. He has had more than 120 books published since 2006. As a newspaper journalist, he won more than 45 awards, including first place for general excellence from the Associated Press. That organization also selected him as one of the top four feature writers in Ohio.